Overview *Ballet*

The world of ballet is explored.

Reading Vocabulary Words

makeup
movements
musicians

High-Frequency Words

practice   *toes*
fit   *families*
learn   *wear*
steps   *lights*

Building Future Vocabulary

* These vocabulary words do not appear in this text. They are provided to develop related oral vocabulary that first appears in future texts.

Words:	*close*	*firm*	*pose*
Levels:	Purple	Turquoise	Library

Comprehension Strategy
Asking questions to understand key themes

Fluency Skill
Adjusting pace

Phonics Skill
Reading simple one-syllable and high-frequency words (of, in, on, and, is, it, the)

Reading-Writing Connection
Writing a paragraph

Home Connection
Send home one of the Flying Colors Take-Home books for children to share with their families.

Differentiated Instruction
Before reading the text, query children to discover their level of understanding of the comprehension strategy — Asking questions to understand key themes. As you work together, provide additional support to children who show a beginning mastery of the strategy.

Focus on ELL

- Show a picture from a ballet. Together point to and discuss the features of the ballet. Help children associate them with the correct English terms.

- Pair children to retell the story. One should read while the other dances like a ballet dancer.

T1

Using This Teaching Version

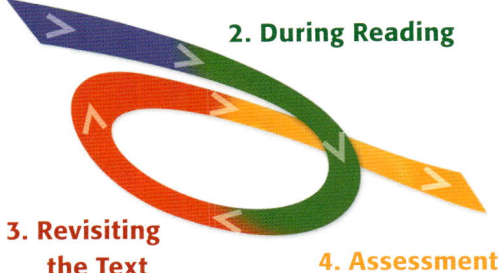

1. Before Reading
2. During Reading
3. Revisiting the Text
4. Assessment

This Teaching Version will assist you in directing children through the process of reading.

1. **Begin with Before Reading** to familiarize children with the book's content. Select the skills and strategies that meet the needs of your children.

2. **Next, go to During Reading** to help children become familiar with the text, and then to read individually on their own.

3. **Then, go back to Revisiting the Text** and select those specific activities that meet children's needs.

4. **Finally, finish with Assessment** to confirm children are ready to move forward to the next text.

1 Before Reading

Building Background

- Write the word *musicians* on the board. Ask children what smaller word they recognize. Underline the word *music*. Ask children what they know about musicians. Correct any misinformation.

- Introduce the book by reading the title, talking about the cover photograph, and sharing the overview.

Building Future Vocabulary
Use Interactive Modeling Card: Same and Opposite

- Introduce the word *close* by writing it in the top box of the Same and Opposite chart.

- Ask *What does it mean when someone is close to something?* (He or she is not very far away from it.) With children, list words that mean the same and opposite of *close* in the appropriate boxes on the chart.

Introduction to Reading Vocabulary

- On blank cards write: *makeup*, *movements*, and *musicians*. Read them aloud. Tell children these words will appear in the text of *Ballet*.

- Use each word in a sentence for understanding.

Introduction to Comprehension Strategy

Use Interactive Modeling Card: Nonfiction Questions and Answers

- Explain that readers often ask questions about what they read. This helps them better understand what they are reading.
- Tell children they will be asking questions to understand key themes in *Ballet*.
- Using the cover photograph, have children develop questions about the book they are about to read.

Introduction to Phonics

- List on the board: **of**, **in**, **on**, **and**, **is**, **it**, **the**. Have children read each word aloud. Point out that these words are in almost every book.
- Have a volunteer come to the board. Ask the volunteer to place a check mark next to each of these words he or she hears as you slowly read aloud page 3. Have another child count how many times each word was marked.
- Repeat the activity with other pages. Have children look for these words as they read.

Modeling Fluency

- Read aloud pages 20 and 21, modeling adjusting reading pace to match the action of the text.
- Talk about how pace can help a reader build excitement in what he or she is reading.

2 During Reading

Book Talk

Beginning on page T4, use the During Reading notes on the left-hand side to engage children in a book talk. On page 24, follow with *Individual Reading*.

During Reading

Book Talk
- Have children look at the title page. Explain to children that the table of contents tells them what each section, or chapter, of the book will be about. It also tells them on which page each chapter begins.

- Discuss the cover photograph and the table of contents. Encourage children to predict what they will learn while reading this book.

- **Comprehension Strategy**
  Before children begin reading, ask them what they already know about ballet. Record their responses on the board.

Turn to page 2 – Book Talk

Revisiting the Text

Ballet

Julie Haydon

Chapter 1	What Is a Ballet?	2
Chapter 2	Learning Ballet	7
Chapter 3	A Ballet Company	12
Chapter 4	Putting on a Ballet	15
Chapter 5	Opening Night	21
Glossary and Index		24

Future Vocabulary

- Explain that a pose is a way of positioning the body. Have children look at the cover photograph. Ask two volunteers to pose like the ballet dancers in the picture. Ask *Is it hard to pose like a ballet dancer?*

- *Is it easier to pose like the man or the woman in this picture?* (the man) *Why?* (The woman is standing on her toes.) *Can you stand on your toes like she does?* (no) *How long do you think it would take to learn to dance on your toes like she is doing?* Ballet dancers train for many years to be able to dance on their toes.

Now revisit pages 4–5

During Reading

Book Talk

- **Comprehension Strategy**
  Direct children's attention to the chapter heading on page 2. Read it aloud. Then model asking questions. Say *I wonder what this chapter of the book will be about. What do you think it will be about?* (what a ballet is and what happens in a ballet) Add questions to the Interactive Modeling Card.

- **Comprehension Strategy**
  Again model asking questions about the text. Have children read the last sentence on page 2. Ask *What do you think the author means when she says,* The story is told without words*?*

- Have children locate the word *makeup* on page 3. Discuss why ballet dancers might wear *makeup*.

Turn to page 4 — Book Talk

Chapter 1
What Is a Ballet?

A ballet is a story told with dance and music. The story is told without words.

Revisiting the Text

The dancers wear **costumes** and makeup.
They dance on a stage.
The stage can be made
to look like different places.

Future Vocabulary
- Explain that *firm* means "stiff" or "not soft." Tell children that ballet dancers have to be strong. Explain that they must have *firm* muscles to be able to dance. Ask *How do you think ballet dancers' muscles become firm?* (The dancers practice and exercise a lot.)

Now revisit pages 4–5

During Reading

Book Talk

- **Comprehension Strategy**
  Direct children's attention to the picture of the costumed goose on page 4. Then model asking questions. Say *I wonder if this ballet is funny, sad, or exciting. What do you think?* (funny) *Why?* (because the goose looks like it is acting funny)

- Point out the boldfaced words on page 5. Explain to children that the boldfaced, or dark, type tells them that the words appear in the glossary at the end of the book. Ask *What is a glossary?* (It is similar to a dictionary; it gives the meanings of the new or difficult words in the book.)

Turn to page 6 – Book Talk

A ballet can be funny, sad, or exciting. Many ballets tell stories about people and animals.

a goose

Revisiting the Text

Some ballets tell **fairy tales** and other stories from books.

Cinderella

Future Vocabulary

- Ask *What are the goose and Cinderella doing?* (They are posing.) *Can you copy their poses?*

- Ask *Do you remember what happens in the story about Cinderella? Why do you think she is posing like this? Is this close to the end of the story or the beginning of the story?* (the beginning) *How do you know?* (She is still in her old clothes; she is not dressed in a ball gown.)

Now revisit pages 6–7

During Reading

Book Talk

- Have children locate the word *movement* on page 6. Have children demonstrate the meaning of the word.

- Point out the chapter heading on page 7. Ask *What does the heading tell you about this chapter?* (that it will be about learning how to dance ballet)

Turn to page 8 – Book Talk

Sometimes a ballet does not tell a story. A ballet can be about how people feel, or it can just have movement and music.

6

Revisiting the Text

Chapter 2
Learning Ballet

Many children learn ballet.
Ballet is fun.
It can help children to be fit and strong.

Future Vocabulary

- Explain that *close* means *near* or *not far*. Ask *Are the ballet dancers on page 6 close to each other?* (yes) *How can you tell?* (because they are holding hands)

- Tell children that ballet dancers must learn many different *pose*s. Ask children to copy the *pose* that the children are doing on page 7. Then ask a volunteer to make up a new ballet *pose* and have the class mimic it. Ask *Do you think it would be hard to learn ballet dancing? Why or why not?*

➥ Now revisit pages 8–9

During Reading

Book Talk

- **Comprehension Strategy**
  Direct children's attention to the picture on page 9 of the ballet dancer on her toes. Ask *What question do you want to ask her about dancing on the tips of her toes?* (Is it hard? Does it hurt? Why do you dance that way?) As appropriate, add questions to the Interactive Modeling Card.

- **Phonics Skill** Refer children to the list of one-syllable words. Have them locate any of these words on page 9. *(the, in, of, on)*

Turn to page 10 — Book Talk

At ballet classes, children learn ballet steps and how to move to music.

8

Revisiting the Text

Older boys and girls learn how to dance together. The girls learn how to dance on the tips of their toes in special ballet shoes.

Future Vocabulary

- Explain that *pose* can also mean *to ask*. Say *If the boy on page 8 were to* pose *a question to the ballet dancers on page 10, what do you think he would ask?* (How long did it take you to learn ballet? What show are you dancing? What do I need to do to be a better ballet dancer?)

Now revisit pages 10–11

During Reading

Book Talk

- **Comprehension Strategy**
  Have children read page 10. Say *I wonder what the author means when she says the dancers use their faces and bodies to tell stories without words. What do you think?* (The dancers smile, frown, look scared, and so on to show what is happening in the story.)

- Ask *How do you think the ballet students feel when they have to dance in front of their families and friends?* (scared, nervous, excited, proud)

- *What questions might you have for these students about learning ballet?* (Is it hard? Do you like it? Does it take a lot of time?)

- Point out that this is the end of Chapter 2. Refer to the Nonfiction Questions and Answers chart. Ask *Can you add any answers to this list?*

Turn to page 12 — Book Talk

Ballet students learn how to use their faces and bodies to tell a story without words.

Revisiting the Text

Most ballet schools put on shows. The ballet students dance in the shows in front of their families and friends.

Future Vocabulary
- Ask *What do the ballet dancer's pose and facial expression on page 10 tell you?* (Something serious is going on; she is sad.)

- **Comprehension Strategy**
Say *Pose a question that you would ask the children in the picture on page 11 about learning ballet.*

Now revisit pages 12–13

During Reading

Book Talk

- Point out that a new chapter begins on page 12. Ask *What is this chapter called?* ("A Ballet Company") *What do you think it will be about?* (a company that puts on ballets)

- Ask children to remind you what the boldfaced type means on page 12. (The word or term appears in the glossary.) Turn to the glossary on page 24 and read aloud the meaning of *ballet company.*

Turn to page 14 – Book Talk

Chapter 3
A Ballet Company

Some ballet students grow up and get work as ballet dancers. Ballet dancers work for a **ballet company**.

12

Revisiting the Text

A ballet company puts on ballets in **theaters**. People pay money to see the ballets.

Future Vocabulary
- Explain that *firm* is also another word for a company or business. Say *For example, a lawyer works at a law firm. A ballet company is like a firm in that many people work together to do a project, or put on a show, that they hope will make money.*

- Ask *Have you ever heard the phrase* to have a firm hand? *What does it mean if we say that someone has a firm hand?* (They are strict or consistent.) *Do you know anyone with a very firm hand?*

Now revisit pages 14–15

During Reading

Book Talk

- **Comprehension Strategy** Ask *What questions might you want to ask about the picture on page 14?* (Does this scene take place before or after the ballet? What is the woman on the right doing? What is her job for the ballet? What is the ballet dancer doing?)

- Point out that Chapter 3 ends on page 14. Ask *Did you learn anything new in this chapter?* Have children add answers to their list of questions.

- Point out that Chapter 4 begins on page 15. Ask *What is the title of Chapter 4?* ("Putting on a Ballet") *What do you think it will be about?* (how a ballet company puts on a ballet)

Turn to page 16 – Book Talk

Ballet dancers are not the only people in a ballet company.
It takes lots of different people to put on a ballet.

Revisiting the Text

Chapter 4
Putting on a Ballet

This is how a ballet company puts on a ballet.

The head of the ballet company chooses the ballet.

Future Vocabulary

- Tell children that *close* can also mean *friendly* or *intimate.* For example, *close* friends spend a lot of time together and know each other well. Ask *Do you think the people who work in a ballet company have to be close?* (yes) *Why or why not?* (They have to be able to work together; they spend a lot of time together practicing and performing.)

Now revisit pages 16–17

During Reading

Book Talk

- **Comprehension Strategy** Remind children that they have read a lot about ballets. Ask *Based on what you know about ballets, what questions can you ask about what you see on these two pages?* (Is the man who is playing the piano making new music for the ballet? What kind of music is he playing? Who is the man helping the ballet dancers? Is he teaching them new dance steps?)

- **Fluency Skill** Point out to children that as the action in the book builds, the pace of their reading should also change. Ask *If the action in the story increases, what should happen to your reading pace?* (It should speed up.) *Why is this important?* (It helps us understand the story better and get more involved in the story.)

Turn to page 18 — Book Talk

Sometimes the head of the ballet company asks for a new ballet to be made.
A new ballet needs a story and new steps.

A new ballet might need new music, too.

16

16

Revisiting the Text

The dancers learn the steps and how to dance them to music.

Future Vocabulary

- Ask *Are the dancers on page 17 close, or near each other?* (yes) *How do you know?* (because their backs are touching) *Do you think they are close friends, too?*

- Ask *Do you think the dancers are enjoying this pose?* (yes) *How can you tell?* (They are smiling.) *What do you enjoy doing?*

Now revisit pages 18–19

During Reading

Book Talk

- Ask children why the word *spare* is in boldfaced type. (because it is in the glossary) Turn to the glossary and have children find the word on the page. Read aloud the definition.

- **Comprehension Strategy**
  Model asking questions to understand key themes. *Say I wonder why ballet dancers wear out so many pairs of shoes. What do you think?* (They wear the shoes a lot; the dance steps wear the shoes out.) *What other questions might you have after reading these pages?* (Why are the laces on ballet shoes so long? How many people does it take to put on a ballet?) As needed, add questions to the Nonfiction Questions and Answers chart.

Turn to page 20 – Book Talk

Costumes are made for the dancers to wear. Dancers wear out lots of ballet shoes, so **spare** shoes are needed.

Revisiting the Text

The stage is set.
Everything on the stage must be easy to move on and off quickly.
The lights are set up.

Future Vocabulary
- **Comprehension Strategy** Say *Pose* a question about something you see in the picture on page 18. (Who are the people in the picture hanging on the wall? Is the woman a ballet dancer or another worker for the ballet company? Whose costume is she working on?)

- Ask *Do the men on page 19 have a firm grip on the item they are carrying?* (One man does, but the other doesn't seem to.)

Now revisit pages 20–21

During Reading

Book Talk

- Have children locate the word *musicians* on page 20. Say *These musicians play in an orchestra. Have you ever heard an orchestra play?*

- **Comprehension Strategy** Say *I wonder why everyone involved in a ballet has to practice so much. What do you think?* (They practice so everything will run smoothly for the performance.) *Do you do anything you need to practice a lot?*

- Point out that page 20 is the end of Chapter 4. With children, add answers to the Nonfiction Questions and Answers chart as appropriate.

- Point out that Chapter 5 begins on page 21. Ask *What do you think this chapter will be about?* (the first night of the ballet) *How do you know?* (The chapter title is "Opening Night.")

Turn to page 22 — Book Talk

The dancers practice and practice.
The musicians practice and practice.

Tickets for the ballet go on sale.

20

20

Revisiting the Text

Chapter 5
Opening Night

It is the **opening night** of the ballet.
The theater is full of people.
The lights go down.

Future Vocabulary

- Say *It is close to the start of the ballet. Pose a question for the dancers as they prepare to go onstage.* (Are you nervous?)

- Say *Pose can also mean pretend. Do you ever pose as someone you are not? Dancers have to pose as a character in performances. Who else poses as a character during a show?* (actors and actresses)

Now revisit pages 22–23

During Reading

Book Talk
- Leave this page spread for children to discover on their own when they read the book individually.

Turn to page 24 — Book Talk

The music starts.

The curtain goes up.
The stage looks wonderful.
The dancers start to dance.

Revisiting the Text

At the end of the ballet,
the **audience** claps.
Everyone at the ballet company
feels very happy.
All the hard work has been worth it!

Future Vocabulary

- Say *Look at the picture on page 22. The dancers are holding very firm poses. How long do you think they can hold this pose?*

- Write *close* on the board and give both pronunciations. Say *The end of the ballet can also be called the close of the ballet. What do you think the dancers will do at the close of the show?* (take a bow) *What do you think the audience will do?* (clap)

- Say *After the audience, the ballet dancers, and everyone else goes home, the last person out will close the doors to the theater. What do you think the dancers will do when they leave?* (go home and rest)

Go to page T5 — Revisiting the Text

During Reading

* Note: Point out this text feature page as a reference point for children's usage while reading independently.

Individual Reading
Have each child read the entire book at his or her own pace while remaining in the group.

Go to page T5 – Revisiting the Text

Glossary

audience	the people who watch a ballet
ballet company	a group of people who put on ballets
costumes	special clothes that dancers wear
fairy tales	stories about make-believe characters
opening night	the first night a ballet is performed
spare	extra, more
theaters	buildings where ballets are performed

Index

ballet company 12, 13, 14, 15, 16, 23
classes 8
costumes 3, 18
music 2, 6, 8, 16, 17, 22
new ballet 16
shoes 9, 18
stage 3, 19, 22
story 2, 4, 5, 6, 16

24

During independent work time, children can read the online book at:
www.rigbyflyingcolors.com

24

Revisiting the Text

Future Vocabulary
- Use the notes on the right-hand pages to develop oral vocabulary that goes beyond the text. These vocabulary words first appear in future texts. These words are: *close*, *firm*, and *pose*.

Turn back to page 1

Reading Vocabulary Review
Activity Sheet: Word Log

- Instruct children to write *makeup*, *movements*, and *musicians* on the Word Log. Point out that each word has a shorter word within it. Have children add the base words to their Word Logs.
- Have children review the text to find the words. Have them define each term in their own words.

Comprehension Strategy Review
Use Interactive Modeling Card: Text Connections Web

- Write the title of the book in the center of the web. Explain that making connections can help us understand and remember what we read.
- Read aloud the list of connection types at the top of the card. With children, fill in the web by making connections to things in the book.

Phonics Review
- Refer children to the list of one-syllable words you wrote on the board. Have them look for those words in the book. *(of, in, and, is, the)*
- Discuss the difficulty in finding these words.

Fluency Review
- Partner children and have them take turns reading Chapter 5, starting on page 21.
- Remind them how to pace their reading to reflect the action that is occurring in the story. As the action on opening night increases, their reading pace should increase as well.

Reading-Writing Connection
Activity Sheet: Nonfiction Questions and Answers

To assist children with linking reading and writing:
- Have children fill in the Nonfiction Questions and Answers chart about what they learned.
- Have children complete and use the Activity Sheet to write a paragraph about ballet.

T5

4 Assessment

Assessing Future Vocabulary

Work with each child individually. Ask questions that elicit each child's understanding of the Future Vocabulary words. Note each child's responses:

- Which of these is closer to Earth: the clouds in the sky or the sun? Why?
- Would you expect a swimmer's muscles to be firm? Why?
- Does it take a lot of practice to learn the poses of ballet?

Assessing Comprehension Strategy

Work with each child individually. Note each child's understanding of asking questions to understand key themes:

- What question might you ask the author of this book? A child who is learning ballet?
- What question might you ask a ballet dancer? The head of a ballet company?
- Was each child able to ask questions that would help him or her better understand the key themes?

Assessing Phonics

Work with each child individually. Note each child's responses for understanding how to read simple one-syllable and high-frequency words:

- Use the following words: *of, in, on, and, is, it, the.*
- Did each child understand that these words contain just one syllable?
- Did each child understand that these words appear often in almost everything he or she reads?

Assessing Fluency

Have each child read page 22 to you. Note each child's understanding of adjusting pace to match the action of what he or she is reading:

- Was each child able to adjust his or her pace to match the action?
- Was each child able to express excitement as the action increased?
- Was each child able to read fluently while quickening his or her reading pace?

Interactive Modeling Cards

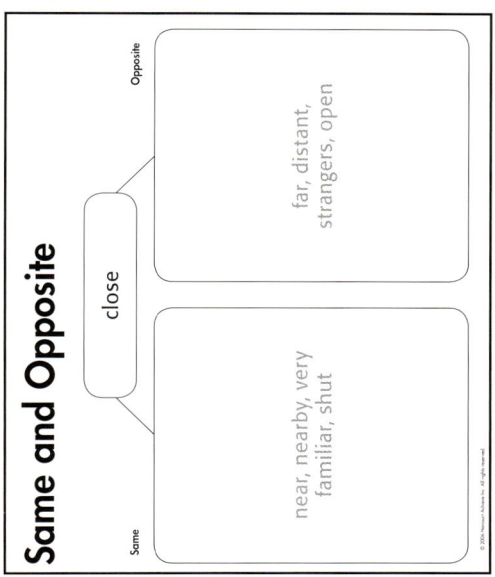 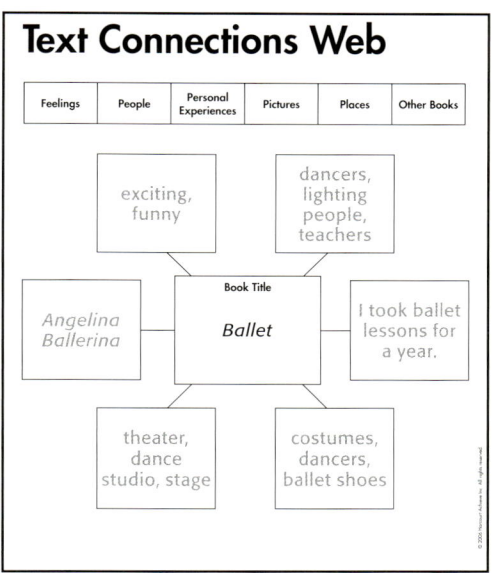

Directions: With children, fill in the Same and Opposite chart using the word *close*.

Directions: With children, fill in the Text Connections Web for *Ballet*.

Discussion Questions

- What was this book about? (Literal)
- What is the hardest part about being a ballet dancer? (Critical Thinking)
- How do you think the members of a ballet company feel at the end of a performance? (Inferential)

Activity Sheets

Word Log

Title: *Ballet*

Word	Meaning from Selection
makeup	stuff you put on your face
make	create
up	opposite of down
movements	actions
move	change the position of the body
musicians	people who play instruments to make music
music	song or tune that goes with the ballet dancing

Directions: Have children fill in the Word Log using the words *makeup*, *make*, *up*, *movements*, *move*, *musicians*, and *music*.

Nonfiction Questions and Answers

Before Reading		During Reading	After Reading
What do I know about this topic?	What do I want to find out by reading this book?	What did I learn?	What new questions do I have?
Ballet is a type of dance.	How do dancers learn ballet?	Ballet takes a lot of practice.	Where can I see a ballet?
People see ballet at theaters.	Is ballet hard to learn?	Some ballets tell fairy tales.	Where can I learn ballet?
Ballet dancers wear costumes.	Who makes the costumes?	Some ballets do not tell a story.	What are famous ballet stories?

Directions: Have children fill in the Nonfiction Questions and Answers chart and use the information to write a paragraph about ballet.

Optional: On a separate sheet of paper, have them make a list of ways to find the answers to the questions they had after reading.